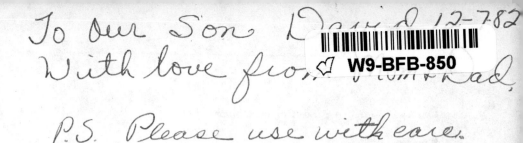

To Our Son David 12-7-82
With love from Mom & Dad,
P.S. Please use with care.

WEIGHT TRAINING FOR BEGINNERS

Bill Reynolds

Contemporary Books, Inc.
Chicago

Library of Congress Cataloging in Publication Data

Reynolds, Bill.
    Weight training for beginners.

    Includes index.
    1. Weight lifting.   I. Title.
GV546.R45   1982   796.4′   82-45444
ISBN 0-8092-5729-7
ISBN 0-8092-5728-9 (pbk.)

Cover photo and all interior photos by John Balik
Models: Carla Neumeier and José Franco

Copyright © 1982 by Contemporary Books, Inc.
All rights reserved
Published by Contemporary Books, Inc.
180 North Michigan Avenue, Chicago, Illinois 60601
Manufactured in the United States of America
Library of Congress Catalog Card Number: 82-45444
International Standard Book Number: 0-8092-5729-7 (cloth)
                                    0-8092-5728-9 (paper)

Published simultaneously in Canada by
Beaverbooks, Ltd.
150 Lesmill Road
Don Mills, Ontario M3B 2T5
Canada

Contents

To Nancy
with affection and gratitude

Foreword

Welcome to the exciting and challenging world of weight training!

By adopting the sensible weight training practices outlined in this book, you can open up numerous new vistas in your life. When I began weight training in my basement in Brooklyn, New York, I was very underweight, introverted, and shy. But through weight training and bodybuilding, I have conquered these problems. I have become an excellent athlete, broken into show business, and been able to make a good living from weight training and bodybuilding.

You probably won't end up playing The Incredible Hulk on television, but you *can* drastically improve your life by regularly training with weights. Whether you are a young man or woman or a more mature man or woman, you will dramatically increase your strength and visibly improve your physical appearance. This in turn will improve your confidence, athletic ability, and self-discipline. In all, I can't recommend weight training to you enough.

Lou Ferrigno, wife Carla, and daughter Shanna Victoria on their way to Italy to film the new HERCULES movie.

I've personally known Bill Reynolds, the author of this book, since 1976, and I've known him through his magazine articles on weight training and bodybuilding for several years longer than that. We have written numerous magazine articles together and share a common philosophy toward weight training. Bill's knowledge of weight training is totally authoritative, and I endorse everything that he has written in this book.

In conclusion, good luck with your weight training workouts. If you train regularly with weights, you will be amazed at how your life will improve!

Lou Ferrigno
Mr. America, Mr. Universe
Film and television star

1

Introduction

One of the most exciting, popular ways to get into optimum physical condition, weight training can produce 10 very positive physical and mental results:

1. Improves health and physical fitness.
2. Shapes and sculptures your body.
3. Optimizes your body weight.
4. Improves sports performance.
5. Relieves the tensions of everyday life.
6. Greatly increases your strength.
7. Increases body flexibility.
8. Fully rehabilitates injuries.
9. Provides a new activity you can do with a girlfriend, boyfriend, and/or family member.
10. Promotes a positive self-image.

All of these benefits are within your reach, virtually no matter what your age. From 9 to 90 years of age, you can

1

receive tremendous benefits from regular and progressive weight training.

By using weight training on a consistent basis, you can harvest tremendous gains in as little as two or three months. From head to toe, your body will begin to look great, and you will develop tremendous strength and drastically improved athletic ability. And as a result of these improvements, you will develop greatly increased self-confidence. In short, with only two or three months of regular and progressive weight training workouts you can become a potential world beater. I've seen it happen to literally hundreds of men and women over the last 20 years.

WHY THIS BOOK?

A beginner to weight training can be easily confused by the huge and bewildering array of potential information sources. Bookstores are loaded with books on weight training, and there are at least ten weight training and bodybuilding magazines available at newsstands. There are also hundreds of "experts" purveying and promoting their surefire methods for improving physical appearance, strength, health, and physical fitness. Unfortunately, less than 10% of the information that you might receive from all of these sources is applicable to a person who is just beginning to exercise with weights.

So, where can a beginner find the type of clearly explained information needed to receive optimum benefits from a self-started weight training program? Essentially, I wrote this book to answer just that question. Through working with beginning weight trainers for nearly twenty years, I've identified a pattern to their questions. Year after year, I've been asked the same questions by each new wave of beginners, and that pattern of questions and the answers to those questions form the framework for this book.

There are numerous scientifically established methods to develop strength, muscle tone, and improved health and physical fitness. And it will be my purpose in this book to explain these tried and proven principles to you in the type of clear language that anyone from 10 to 100 years of age can easily understand. So, by reading this book and following my recommendations to the letter, you can have the maximum chance of reaching your goals through weight training!

WHAT IS WEIGHT TRAINING?

Weight training, sometimes called *progressive resistance exercise*, is a form of muscular exercise that uses the resistance provided by free weights (barbells and dumbbells) or various types of exercise machines. Within the basic definition of weight training, there are four specific types of resistance exercise.

Bodybuilding

Often this is a form of competition in which heavy weight training is used to develop large and well-defined muscles. Both men and women compete in bodybuilding. More commonly, though, bodybuilding merely consists of trying to trim down a pudgy part of the body or to build up an area that is too skinny.

Weight Lifting

This is another form of competitive weight training that consists of attempting to lift the heaviest weight with well-defined movements. There are two types of weight lifting: Olympic-style weight lifting and powerlifting.

Athletic Training

Most athletes use some form of weight training to increase strength. In general, a stronger athlete is a better athlete.

Injury Rehabilitation

Weight training is widely recommended by sports medicine experts to strengthen injury-weakened joints and muscles, once those injuries have healed.

HOW IT WORKS

The human body is a remarkable organism. Every external stimulus evokes from it a distinct physical response. Eat trashy, devitalized, overrefined food, for example, and your body will grow weak, fat, and flaccid. If you eat natural, wholesome, and vitally healthy foods, however, your body will grow lean, strong, and healthy in response. You can also make your body become flaccid, sluggish, and unattractive simply by avoiding physical activity. Lie in front of a television set for 12–14 hours per day—munching potato chips and swilling beer—and you will quickly reach this state. Or, you can stimulate your body to become lean, hard, and physically fit simply by making regular and vigorous exercise an integral part of your lifestyle.

To reach your goals of better appearance and buoyantly good health, you must provide your body with as many beneficial stimuli as possible. By improving your diet a little, engaging in moderate aerobic exercise and regular stretching workouts, and adopting a program of progressively intensified resistance exercise, you will be providing enough positive stimulation to result in a new you in record time!

MUSCLE PHYSIOLOGY

Like the body as a whole, the muscles respond in specific ways to specific stimuli. In the case of weight training, when a muscle group is overloaded (i.e., stressed by a load greater than what it is used to handling), it responds by growing in size, strength, and muscle tone. Physiologists call this *muscle hypertrophy*, and the principle is unchanged regardless of the organism involved. All types of animals—not just humans—respond to this type of overload conditioning with increased muscle mass and strength.

To illustrate how this phenomenon works, review the case of Joe and Jane Weight Trainer. Let's assume that in a Squat movement (doing a Deep Knee Bend with a barbell across the shoulders) Joe can do six repetitions with 75 pounds in his first workout, and Jane can do six reps with 50 pounds.

In both cases these weights are heavier than the lifters are used to. Consequently, their muscles grow larger, stronger, and better toned. As a result, in the second workout Joe does six reps at 80 pounds in the Squat and Jane manages 55 pounds for six reps. As true believers in weight training, Joe and Jane push onward: he uses 85 pounds for six reps in his third training session, and she uses 60 pounds for her six repetitions. Clearly, both are significantly stronger now than when they started training with weights.

By consistently and progressively overloading their muscles in a variety of weight training movements, both Joe and Jane can make tremendous progress in strength and physical development in one year. Joe will eventually be able to squat for six reps with 320 pounds, which is 400 percent better than what he started with. And Jane will be capable of squatting for six repetitions with 200 pounds, a full 400-percent improvement.

These are no small accomplishments, but they are also by no means out of the ordinary. One athlete I knew was consistently able to high-jump 6'2". I put him on a progressive weight training program. During his initial workout he could squat 75 pounds for 10 reps. But during almost every workout for nearly a year he added 5 to 10 pounds to his workout weight for the Squat until he could do 10 repetitions with 375 pounds. While he gained only two or three pounds of body weight, he cracked 7'0" in the high jump by the end of the year. Only death in a car crash kept him from eventually making an Olympic team.

Overall, muscle size and strength are directly proportionate to the amount of weight you use in various weight training movements. And since it is relatively easy to increase training poundages, it is a simple matter to gain strength and improve athletic ability, health, and physical appearance and to optimize body weight through weight workouts.

MYTHS

It's simply astounding how many idiotic myths exist about weight training and bodybuilding. And the odd part is that, even though thousands of men and women continue to cling to these myths, science has for the most part disproved every one. Still, let's debunk the six major myths associated with training with weights.

1. *Weight training makes you muscle-bound.* Nothing could be further from the truth. Beginning in 1950, scores of scientific studies have proved the opposite: weight training actually improves muscle and joint flexibility.

2. *Weight training stunts growth.* Actually, any type of regular exercise, including weight training, stimulates a height increase. Typical of the many tall bodybuilders is 6'5" Lou Ferrigno, star of "The Incredible Hulk" television show. While weight training may not have actually *caused* him to grow to such a height, it certainly didn't stunt his growth.

3. *Weight training will make a woman unfeminine.* On the contrary, women who train with weights tend to develop incredibly shapely, firm, and sexy bodies. Take a good look at the female model used to illustrate the exercises in this book, because she has trained steadily with weights for more than two years. I'm certain that you will agree that she is a picture of femininity.

4. *Muscle tissue turns to fat as soon as a man or woman ceases weight training.* This is totally absurd, because, physiologically, it's completely impossible for muscle tissue to

turn into fat. When weight training is terminated, muscles merely atrophy, or slowly return to their original size.

5. *Weight training ruins the back, knees, and other joints.* In point of fact, when it is done correctly, weight training actually improves the strength and health of all of the body's joints. Far fewer weight trainers than runners have joint injuries.

6. *Weight training slows a person down.* If this myth were fact, no athlete would train with weights. Instead, virtually all athletes work out with weights, Nautilus machines, and other resistance apparatus. It's a fact that there is a direct relationship between muscle strength and speed of movement.

PROS AND CONS OF WEIGHT TRAINING

As with all types of exercise, there are both advantages and disadvantages to weight training. Fortunately, every disadvantage can be neutralized. Since the advantages of weight training far outweigh the disadvantages, let's start by briefly describing the disadvantages.

Disadvantages

1. *Weight training can be boring.* Because of the inherent repetitious nature of weight training, it *can* be boring. But if training routines are changed frequently, it is possible to reduce or eliminate such boredom. Lou Ferrigno actually changes his training schedule daily.

2. *Weight training develops little significant aerobic endurance.* This is quite true, but a weight training program can easily be combined with running, swimming, cycling, or some other type of aerobic activity. In fact, interspersing aerobic routines among weight training sets can help alleviate boredom, too. And although weight training is a valuable component of a total fitness program, it is intended

to develop primarily strength and muscle tone, not en-durance.

3. *Everyone—male and female—will gain some degree of muscular body weight from weight training.* Putting an overload stress on any skeletal muscle will cause it to hyper-trophy. But muscle mass gains from weight training are advantageous, because such a weight gain is functional and more than carries itself in physical activities. In short, it's something to be welcomed, not scorned. And, as will soon be explained in detail, a woman will achieve a markedly lesser degree of muscle mass gain through weight training than will any man.

Advantages

1. *Selectivity.* With weight training you can do exercises that stress specific muscle groups in isolation from the rest of the body. In some cases even small segments of a muscle group can be stressed. This factor is very important in using weights to rehabilitate injuries.

2. *Unlimited range of resistance.* You can do weight train-ing exercises with as little as one pound of resistance or with as many as 1,000 pounds. No other type of exercise offers such a wide range of resistance.

3. *Optimizes body weight.* In combination with diet, weight training makes it easy to gain or lose body weight until you reach your optimum weight.

4. *Fast strength gains.* No other physical activity can strengthen the body's muscles as quickly, or to as great a degree, as weight training.

MEN vs. WOMEN

While men have been weight training in America for nearly a century, mass use of weights by women is a rela-tively new phenomenon. Fortunately, there are very few other differences between the sexes that apply to weight training. Women can train as long and as hard as men, but they will generally be weaker and will develop feminine curves from weight workouts, not the more massive and well-defined muscles of men.

The difference between men and women is basically hormonal. While both men and women secrete the hormones testosterone and estrogen, men produce quite high levels of the male muscle-building hormone testosterone. Women, on the other hand, secrete primarily estrogen, which gives them soft curves and precludes the development of large muscles.

Even though men are stronger than women, women generally have equal or greater endurance. And women have much higher pain thresholds. Therefore, a women can easily and safely perform the same number of exercises, sets, and repetitions as her male counterpart. The only concession she must make when training with a man is to use lighter weights in each exercise.

THE AGE FACTOR

There are no particular age limitations for weight training. Children as young as six or seven have trained safely with weights, though a younger child usually won't have a long enough attention span to work out consistently. I've known both men and women in their seventies and eighties—and even an old fellow of 96—who weight trained, and I know literally hundreds in their fifties and sixties who work out. It's never too late to start weight training!

I'm often asked what the ideal age is at which to start a weight training program. Since it's an excellent idea to exercise at any age, weight training can and should be started by every man and woman, regardless of age. Still, men and women between the ages of 15 and 25 have the best combination of both maturity and youth to make the fastest gains from progressive resistance exercise.

THE BEAUTY OF IT

After more than twenty years of training, five years of teaching weight training on the college level, and working as a weight training and bodybuilding magazine writer and editor for nearly fifteen years, I feel I can speak with authority about the real beauty of weight training. I can tell you why millions of men and women—myself included—have "iron fever," our way of saying they are totally addicted (in a positive sense, of course) to pumping iron.

First, weight training provides you with incredibly fast and dramatic results. You will feel a significant strength increase between your first and second workouts. Your muscles will be harder to the touch, and you will even be able to see small changes in the shape and form of your body.

Secondly, you alone are responsible for your successes and failures in weight training. In other words, no one else can do the workouts for you; you have to do them yourself. You get out of weight training exactly what you put into it. You succeed or fail in the long run entirely on your own merits, so after one or two doses of "iron pills" you, too, might very well end up hooked for life!

2

Techniques

Now that you know what weight training is all about and what to expect from it, we can move on to the basic techniques. This is the most important chapter in this book, because it contains all the information that will allow you to train with weights safely and successfully. Before you actually begin to work out with weights, it is essential that you master the techniques outlined in this chapter.

BASIC TERMINOLOGY

There are several fundamental terms that you should understand thoroughly before you begin home-gym training, and definitely before you decide to crash an organized weight room.

An *exercise* (also referred to as a *movement*) is the full movement—such as a Push-Up or a Bench Press—that you do when training with weights. Many exercises are done in one weight training workout.

11

A *repetition* (often abbreviated to *rep*) is each full cycle of the movement of an exercise. As an example of a repetition, a full rep in a Squat (a Deep Knee Bend with a barbell rested across the shoulders) would start with the legs straight and the body erect. Then, with the torso held upright, the legs would be fully bent, then fully straightened to arrive back at the starting point. This cycle is one repetition.

A *set* is a distinct grouping of consecutive repetitions for any exercise, usually from a minimum of 5–6 reps up to a maximum of 15–20 (except for abdominal exercises, which are often done in sets of up to 100 reps). Multiple sets are usually performed for each exercise in a workout.

Between sets, a *rest interval* of 30–90 seconds is taken. This is just a rest break that allows your muscles to recuperate partially before the next set is begun.

A *workout*—alternatively called a *routine, program*, or *training program*—is the entire schedule of exercises, sets, and repetitions done in one session of weight training each day.

An *overgrip* is a type of grip on a barbell handle in which the palms face the body when you hold a barbell and stand erect with your arms at your sides. An *undergrip* is one in which the palms point away from the body in this stance. At times a *mixed grip* is used, in which one hand is held in an overgrip and the other in an undergrip position.

EQUIPMENT ORIENTATION

The basic piece of weight training equipment is a *barbell,* illustrated in Figure 1, with each of its parts labeled.

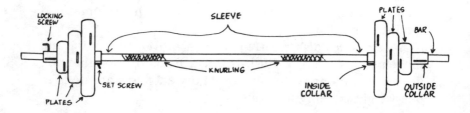

Barbell *bars* vary in length from four to six feet, and they generally weigh approximately five pounds per foot with the collars in place. This base weight must be taken in consideration when adding plates to the bar to form a desired training poundage.

The *sleeve* of a barbell is a hollow metal tube fitted over the bar, so the bar can rotate more freely in the hands. *Knurlings* are grooves scored into the sleeve. They make it easier to grasp a barbell with sweaty hands in the middle of a workout. *Plates* are made from either cast iron or concrete-filled vinyl casings. The metal plates are best. They are far more durable, and you can load a barbell to a far heavier weight with metal plates than with the bulkier vinyl ones.

Dumbbells are short-handled barbells, usually 12–16 inches long. They are intended for use in pairs, one held in each hand. In large organized gyms, dumbbells and barbells are fixed, or have the plates bolted or welded semipermanently in place. Several racks of such fixed barbells and dumbbells eliminate the time-consuming necessity of changing the plates on a barbell or two dumbbells between exercises.

In the photos with the exercise descriptions in Chapter 3, you will note that an *exercise bench* is used. These benches come in several varieties, the best of which has an adjustable board that allows you to vary widely the bench's angle of incline. Many other types of specialized benches also exist, and you will understand their use as you progress in your experience with weight training.

PHYSICAL EXAMS

While most men and women reading this book will be in their teens and twenties, a few will be older. Anyone who is under 30 years of age and who has been exercising at least one day per week for the past year can safely avoid having a physical examination prior to commencing weight training. But if you are over 30 or have been physically inactive for at least the last year, it is essential that you have your family physician give you a thorough physical exam. And if you are over 40, this physical should also include an electrocardiogram (EKG) stress test.

A physician can detect existing or impending heart and other problems during the course of a thorough physical examination. And while such problems won't necessarily prevent you from commencing a program of weight training, they may require you to approach the activity more slowly and conservatively than I will recommend in the balance of this book. In any event, you should strictly follow the advice of your physician whenever it differs from my recommendations.

PROGRESSION

Progression is the heart and soul of weight training. As you will recall, a muscle grows stronger, larger, and better toned when subjected to strong resistance. But muscles grow used to a particular load very quickly, and you must soon place even greater stress on a muscle to keep it growing.

To progressively increase the amount of resistance on an exercise, we gradually increase the number of repetitions done on an exercise, starting with a specific *lower guide number* and working up to an *upper guide number*. Then we add 5–10 pounds of resistance to the exercise and begin with reps at the lower guide number, again gradually working back to the upper guide number.

It is usually possible to add at least 10 pounds on movements that affect such large muscle groups as the legs and back. For the smaller muscle areas, however, it will be possible to add only five pounds each time new resistance is placed on a group of muscles with an exercise.

To clearly illustrate this process of progression, let's say that you must do one set of Bench Presses for 8–12 repetitions. In this case 8 is the lower guide number, and 12 is the upper guide number. Over a period of four weeks, you might progressively work upward in your training resistance in the following manner (40 × 8 means *forty pounds for eight repetitions*):

	Day 1	Day 2	Day 3
Week 1	40 × 8	40 × 9	40 × 10
Week 2	40 × 11	40 × 12	45 × 8
Week 3	45 × 9	45 × 10	45 × 11
Week 4	45 × 12	50 × 8	50 × 9

In most exercises you will be required to do more than one set, usually three or four. In such a case you should reach the upper guide number for every set before increasing your training poundage. Assuming that you must do three sets of 8–12 repetitions in the Barbell Bent Rowing exercise, here is a four-week sample progression for that movement:

	Day 1	Day 2	Day 3
Week 1	50 × 8	50 × 10	50 × 11
	50 × 8	50 × 9	50 × 10
	50 × 8	50 × 8	50 × 10
Week 2	50 × 12	50 × 12	50 × 12
	50 × 11	50 × 12	50 × 12
	50 × 10	50 × 11	50 × 12
Week 3	55 × 9	55 × 11	55 × 12
	55 × 8	55 × 10	55 × 11
	55 × 8	55 × 10	55 × 10
Week 4	55 × 12	55 × 12	60 × 8
	55 × 12	55 × 12	60 × 8
	55 × 10	55 × 12	60 × 8

Proper weight training progression is a slow, steady procedure. But if you try hard to add one or two new reps to each movement during every workout, you will soon be using very heavy weights in every exercise. Laura Combes, an

American Women's Bodybuilding Champion, has bench pressed 185 pounds for 8 reps at a body weight of 125 pounds. And 200-pound Tim Belknap, a Mr. America winner, has squatted with 675 pounds for 10 reps. With proper progression in your weight training workouts, you will find that your muscles can continue to grow stronger and stronger year after year, until you can lift at least two or three times more weight in every exercise than you could originally handle. Some men who are genetically gifted for strength development have increased their poundage in some exercises by a factor of more than ten.

TRAINING SPEED

As you go through the suggested weight training programs in Chapter 4, it is best to do all of the required sets of an exercise before proceeding to the next movement. And between sets of an exercise—as well as between movements— you will need to take a rest.

The length of such rest intervals is important. In this book I suggest that you pause for 60 seconds between sets. You could rest for as few as 30 seconds, but such short rest intervals don't allow you to use maximum exercise weights for each set. And if you rest for more that 60–90 seconds between sets, it is possible for your body to cool down as your workout progresses, leaving you open to injury.

TRAINING FREQUENCY

Muscles don't grow in size, strength, and tone while you are actually training them. Instead, this happens while you rest between exercise sessions. It takes about 48–60 hours for a muscle group to recuperate (fully rest, remove fatigue by-products, and restore muscle sugar supplies) and grow. Therefore, it's best to rest one full day or more between training days.

For our purposes, it is best to train on three nonconsecutive days each week. This can be Monday, Wednesday, and Friday; Tuesday, Thursday, and Saturday; or any other combination you can think of that fits into your schedule. Because it leaves weekends free for other recreational pursuits, most individuals who weight train seem to prefer the Monday-Wednesday-Friday schedule.

After about six months of steady training you can switch to what is called a *split routine*. In such a program you divide the muscle groups of your body into halves (e.g., the upper body and lower body are two halves) and train one half on Mondays and Thursdays, the other on Tuesdays and Fridays. A split routine allows you to do longer workouts for each body part without generally overtraining.

WHEN TO TRAIN

There is no set time of day to train with weights, though most serious weight trainers seem to work out in either the morning or the late afternoon. Simply fit your workouts into your schedule whenever it is best for you.

If you do some type of aerobic training or participate in a sport, it's best to weight train at least one hour before or after the other activity. Similarly, you should never eat within an hour of starting or finishing a workout. Meal digestion requires a great supply of blood, which will be drained from the rest of the body including the muscles.

WHERE TO TRAIN

The best place for most men and women—particularly beginners—to train with weights is in a home gym. Such a gym can be set up in a basement, garage, or any other area in which you can find a six-by-six space with a ceiling at least eight feet high.

Home-gym training offers privacy, no crowds, a chance to

train at any convenient hour of the day or night (organized gyms have set hours) at a lower cost than a gym or spa membership. For under $200 you can fully equip a home gym. Once equipped, the gym will cost you little to maintain. A one-year spa membership costs roughly twice as much as setting up a home gym, and it must be paid year after year. In Chapter 6, I will tell you where to buy equipment for a home gym, as well as what pieces to purchase.

If you become particularly serious—you want to improve your sports performance to an Olympian level, you want to become a bodybuilder, or you decide you like competitive weight lifting—you must ultimately move out of your home gym and into one of the high-quality professional gyms dotting America, or perhaps into a high school or college weight room. There you will have a far greater variety of equipment, as well as the comradeship of other competitive athletes.

Gyms such as I just described are listed in your telephone directory yellow pages under "Gyms" or "Health Clubs."

WHAT TO WEAR

Clothing for weight training should be loose and/or elastic enough to allow a complete range of motion for each limb. It should also be thick enough to keep the body from cooling off during a workout in a cold or drafty gym. Several thin layers of clothing will keep the body warmer than one thick layer, because multiple layers trap insulating air between them.

Shorts and a T-shirt are the usual training attire for both men and women. Men can wear an athletic supporter and women a bra, if either is desired. In cooler climates a sweatsuit can be added.

Both men and women should wear socks and shoes while weight training. Running shoes are quite appropriate, because they have a good skid-preventing tread and built-in arch supports. These arch supports will help protect the arches of your feet from injuries (such as fallen arches) that might occur if your foot is structurally weak and you lift very heavy weights while barefooted.

WEIGHT LIFTING BELTS

Large leather weight lifting belts are often used by weight trainers, bodybuilders, and competitive weightlifters. They are generally made of leather about ⅛-¼ inch thick, and they are either four or six inches wide across the back. They are available through bodybuilding and weight training magazines, as well as at many sporting goods stores.

Fastened tightly around the waist, weight lifting belts protect the stomach and lower back from injury while you are using heavy weights. They are particularly valuable when doing Squats, overhead lifts (e.g., Military Presses), and back work (e.g., Deadlifts, Bent Rowing, etc.).

STARTING WEIGHTS

The amount of weight you use for each exercise will depend on how naturally strong you are (to a great degree, any man's or woman's strength levels—especially in terms of the ultimate strength levels that can be developed—are determined by one's genetic makeup) and how physically active you have been in recent years. As a result, starting weights (often called *poundages*) will vary from one person to another, and it's difficult to predict exactly what starting weight you should use for each movement.

Still, for the beginning routine in Chapter 4, I will recommend starting weights in terms of percentage of your body weight. There will be two columns, marked "% Men" and "% Women," for this purpose, and all you will need to do to determine your exercise weight is to multiply your body weight by the appropriate %.

Once you have trained with weights for a few weeks, you will be able to determine the correct poundages for each movement on your own. A weight that is too light allows you to easily do the required number of repetitions, while a weight that is too heavy forces you to uncomfortably struggle to reach your rep goal. A correct exercise poundage is one that makes it comfortably difficult to do a desired number of repetitions for an exercise.

HOW MANY REPS?

For the upper body muscle groups (chest, back, shoulders, upper arms) you should keep your reps in the range of 8–12, while you should do 10–15 reps per set for your thigh muscles. Your abdominal muscles require 25–100 reps per set, and your calves and forearms will normally respond best to 15–20 reps each set.

You might well wonder why the number of reps varies so widely from muscle group to muscle group. There are two reasons for this: (1) Some muscle groups have a greater content of endurance-promoting fibers (called *slow-twitch muscle fibers*), while others have a greater content of strength-promoting fibers (called *fast-twitch muscle fibers*); and (2) Muscles, such as the calves and forearms, that are used frequently throughout the day, are composed of muscle fibers that have been toughened to exercise and thus require the stimulation of relatively high reps with heavy training weights.

EXERCISE FORM

Weight training movements are designed to put stress on specific muscle groups. And they can only do this if you are careful to move only those parts of your body specified for each exercise. Using other parts of the body to jerk or swing a weight up to the finish position is called "cheating," and it only robs the muscle groups being trained by an exercise of much of the stress that they should be receiving.

In each weight training exercise it is also essential to move the barbell or dumbbells over the complete range of motion of the body joints involved. A working muscle should be moved under heavy resistance from full extension to full contraction and back to full extension on every repetition of an exercise. Shorter movements also rob a working muscle of some of the stress—and hence some of the development—it should receive from an exercise.

BREATHING

There is undue concern among all beginning trainees—and even among many advanced participants—about how to breathe correctly while doing a weight training movement. Actually, it makes no difference when you breathe during an exercise, as long as you do breathe in and out enough during the movement to keep from passing out.

Under no circumstances should you hold your breath during a movement, however. This is particularly true when doing Bench Presses with a heavy weight. Holding your breath impedes blood flow to and from the brain, which induces a Valsalva effect, resulting in a momentary blackout. If you black out while pushing up a heavy barbell in a Bench Press, the bar could easily crash down on your neck, killing you.

When doing a weight training movement, let nature help you decide when to breathe. In each movement there are points at which it is easiest to breathe in and out, and you will automatically inhale and exhale at these points. If you feel that you *must* be bound by a rule for breathing, it's safest to breathe in during the relaxation phase of a movement and out as you exert.

SLEEP AND REST

A muscle will grow in size, strength, and tone only if it fully recuperates between workouts. Such recuperation takes 48–60 hours, but merely letting 48–60 hours elapse between sessions doesn't ensure full recuperation. You must not only refrain from working out with weights while your muscles are recuperating, but also be sure that you rest periodically throughout the day and get sufficient sleep.

Resting involves allowing yourself two or three 15- to 30-minute rest breaks spaced out evenly during the day whenever you are working especially hard or are otherwise overly stressed. During such a break you should lie down or partially recline on a soft surface and allow yourself to unwind mentally and physically. You will be surprised at how quickly and completely such rest breaks will recharge your energy batteries.

Individual sleep requirements vary widely. Some individuals can function perfectly on only four or five hours of sleep a day, while others act like zombies if they get less than 10–12 hours of sound sleep each night. Generally speaking, eight hours per night is the right amount of sleep for most people, but you will need to experiment to decide how much sleep you need. Be sure, however, to get enough sleep each night to allow yourself to be alert and energetic the next day.

NUTRITION

Scores of books and hundreds of magazine articles have been written about the relationship between nutrition and exercise. Unfortunately, all of this clouds the issue for a beginning weight trainer, because it doesn't make much difference whether you're a pure carnivore or a strict vegetarian when it comes to making progress from weight training workouts. Nor do you need to chuck down a hundred vitamin pills and a pound of protein powder every day.

Simply eat a balanced diet with plenty of fresh fruits and vegetables. Consume approximately ½ gram of protein from dietary sources per pound of your body weight and try to avoid "junk" foods made from refined grains and sugars. Finally, if you feel you need extra vitamins and minerals in your diet, take one multiple vitamin-mineral tablet per day, preferably with a meal. Both vitamins and minerals are more efficiently used by the human body if they are taken with regular food.

THE MENTAL ASPECTS

Weight trainers and bodybuilders often refer to the human mind as the body's "master organ," because it controls—either consciously or subconsciously—all of the voluntary and involuntary processes of the body. By consciously seeking to strengthen the link between your mind and working muscles while training with weights, you'll get much more out of your workouts. There are three mental techniques you can use to improve your chances of success in weight training.

First, you should concentrate solely on the muscles being worked. Think about the biceps muscles contracting and extending while you do a Barbell Curl. The better you concentrate, the greater will be your gains from weight training.

Second, always be positive in your thinking about your training and results you will receive from it. The more certain you are that you will succeed, the greater chance that you really will succeed.

Finally, create a mental image of how you eventually want to look, how strong you will be, and how much better will be your athletic ability. Use this visualization process regularly and you will soon attain the images you conjure up in your mind.

BREAKING IN

Weight training very severely stresses untrained muscles, so jumping into a full workout program during your first training session can make virtually every muscle in your body extremely sore. With a gradual introduction to heavy resistance training over a 4–6-week period, however, muscle soreness can be avoided completely or at least kept to a minimum.

The best way to begin is to do only one light set of each exercise in your recommended routine during your first workout or two. Then gradually add one or two total sets to your workout schedule in each training session for two or three weeks until you are doing the entire program. Once you have reached this point, you can go all out trying to progressively increase the resistance you use in each movement.

Even with this type of slow and gradual entry into weight training, you may experience mild to moderate muscle soreness. Many remedies to this have been suggested, but in my experience the best remedy is frequent long, hot baths.

WARM-UPS

Most likely, weight training is a heavier and more stressful activity than anything you have ever done before. And without a good full-body warm-up, it's quite possible that you will eventually injure yourself while weight training. At the very least you will become stiff and sore if you don't warm up before using heavy weights in your workout. Once you are warmed up, however, you won't incur an injury if you can maintain a fast pace in your workout.

An ideal preworkout warm-up should last about 10–15 minutes. Start with 3–5 minutes of jumping rope or vigorously jogging in place. After that, spend 5–10 minutes doing progressively more strenuous calisthenics and stretching movements. This amount of calisthenics and stretching will make you feel warm and slightly sweaty, and if you measure your pulse rate, you'd see that it has gone up 20–30 beats per minute. At this point, conclude your workout by doing one light set of 20 reps in the Squat, Bench Press, and Barbell Bent Rowing movements.

After this type of warm-up you will be ready to tackle even the heaviest weights safely.

SAFETY

Generally speaking, weight training is a very safe activity, but serious injuries can occur if proper safety procedures are not followed. Therefore, it is essential that you become fully aware of each of the safety rules proposed in this section. My friend Lou Ferrigno, a Mr. America and Mr. Universe winner who portrayed The Incredible Hulk on television for five years, offers these 12 weight training safety rules:

1. *Use spotters.* Spotters are training partners who stand by to rescue you when a barbell pins you to a bench or to the floor. Spotters are essential when doing heavy Bench Presses and Squats.

2. *Never train alone.* Even though this is a difficult rule to follow when home-gym training, someone should always be available to spot you. If possible, this person should be an advanced weight trainer who can monitor your exercise form in the initial stages of your training.

3. *Use catch racks.* Organized gyms have special racks to catch an errant barbell during heavy movements like Squats and Bench Presses.

4. *Use collars.* If the plates slide off one end of a barbell during heavy movements like Squat and Bench Presses, it can wrench your back, knees, wrists, elbows, or shoulders.

5. *Never hold your breath.* You could pass out.

6. *Maintain good gym housekeeping.* Loose barbells, dumbbells, and plates on the floor of a gym can trip someone and cause an injury.

7. *Train under competent supervision.* A good coach can keep you from developing dangerous exercise habits.

8. *Don't train in an overcrowded gym.* If you are forced to wait too long for a piece of equipment, your body can cool down. And, as mentioned earlier, a cooling muscle is easily injured.

9. *Always warm up thoroughly.* In effect, this is the same as rule 8. Warm up your body thoroughly and then keep up a good exercise pace.

10. *Use proper biomechanical positionings (body positions) in all exercises.* These are included in all of the written and photographic descriptions in this book, so be careful not to deviate from the performance method recommended for each movement.

11. *Use a weight lifting belt.* Such belts protect the lower back and abdomen from injury. The subject of weight lifting belts is covered in more detail earlier in this chapter.

12. *Acquire as much knowledge as possible about weight training.* If you are well-informed, it will be much easier to avoid injuries.

WHEN TO CHANGE ROUTINES

The human body is very adaptable, and within a few weeks it becomes so used to a particular weight training routine that it begins to respond more and more slowly. Additionally, staying on a routine too long can lead to boredom, which also slows progress.

To keep progressing quickly, it's best to switch to a new training routine every four to six weeks. This allows your mind and body to tackle the new workout program with greater enthusiasm and receptiveness, thus allowing you to make faster progress.

3

Exercises

The 30 exercises described in detail and clearly illustrated in this chapter represent only a small fraction of all those movements available for use in weight training. Still, they are the most commonly used weight training exercises, and you will use most of them from time to time for as long as you exercise with weights. Therefore, each of these 30 movements should be fully mastered.

These basic exercises will also provide you with a good starting point in your quest to develop a more complete pool of 75 to 100 movements from which to choose your workouts as you become more and more advanced in weight training. To these 30 movements, you will be able over the years to add scores of other exercises that you discover in reading more advanced weight training books and magazines, or while working out in a public gym and carefully observing other men and women training with weights.

The **Clean and Press** is an excellent warm-up exercise, because it stresses virtually every muscle group in the body.

It is also a good illustration of how to lift any heavy weight from the floor correctly and safely.

Stand next to the middle of the handle of a barbell that is lying on the floor at your feet. Your feet should be set at shoulder width, your toes must point forward, and your shins should be only one to two inches from the barbell handle. Bend over and take an overgrip on the barbell with each hand set two to three inches wider than your shoulders. Bend your knees, flatten your back, keep your arms straight, and look directly ahead. In this position, your back should be at about a 45-degree angle to the floor, your hips should be above your knees, and your shoulders should be above your hips.

From this starting position, rapidly pull the bar from the floor to your shoulders, keeping it close to your body at all times. This pulling movement is accomplished by first straightening your legs, then your back. Finally, you should follow through by pulling with your arms and then whipping your elbows under the bar to secure the barbell at your shoulders. This movement is called a **Power Clean**.

Next, move your elbows directly under the barbell handle and then straighten your arms to push the weight directly overhead until it is at arms' length. This movement is called a **Military Press**, and it is described in greater detail later in this chapter.

Lower the weight back to the starting point on the floor by reversing the procedure described for raising it. Repeat the movement for the required number of repetitions.

The **Squat** is a superior thigh, buttock, and lower back exercise.

Place a barbell across your shoulders behind your neck and balance it in position by grasping the barbell handle out toward the plates on each side. Stand with your feet set at shoulder width, your toes pointed outward at 45-degree angles. Tighten all of the muscles of your back and keep them tensed throughout the movement.

Clean and Press—Start.

Midpoint 1.

Midpoint 2.

Finish.

Squat—Start.   Squat—Finish.

Keeping your torso as erect as possible, fully bend your legs. As you sink down into the squatting position, your knees should travel outward directly over your feet. Do not bounce at the bottom of the movement. Slowly straighten your legs and return to the starting point. Repeat the movement.

If you have difficulty squatting flat-footed (a sign of ankle inflexibility), stand with your heels resting on a two-by-four-inch board or book when you do Squats.

The **Iron Boot Leg Extension** directly stresses the quadriceps muscles along the front of your thighs.

Place a dumbbell handle through the holes in the sole of the boot, then load an appropriate number of plates on the bar. Strap the boot on your foot. (It will be rather painful to do this barefooted, so be sure to wear athletic shoes.) Sit at the edge of a high bench or table with your knee at the edge of it. Hang your shin and the boot directly downward so your exercising leg is bent at a 90-degree angle.

From this starting position, slowly straighten your leg. Pause for a count of two at the top position. Then lower the boot back to the starting position. Repeat for the required number of repetitions and be sure that you do an equal number of sets and reps for each leg.

The **Iron Boot Leg Curl** strongly stimulates the hamstring muscles along the back of your thighs.

Load up the boot and strap it on one foot. Stand erect with your nonexercising foot on a four-by-four-inch block of wood or a couple of thick books. Grasp a tabletop, an upright pole, or some other object to balance your body during the movement. Press your thighs together.

From this starting position, slowly bend your leg and curl the foot with the boot in a semicircle, starting with your leg

Leg Extension—Start.

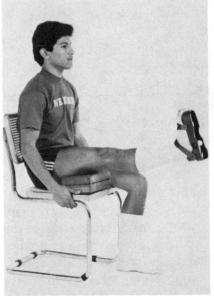
Leg Extension—Finish.

perfectly straight and finishing when your working leg is as fully bent as possible. Pause for a second at the top of the movement, then lower back to the starting position. Repeat the movement. Be sure to do an equal number of sets and reps for each leg.

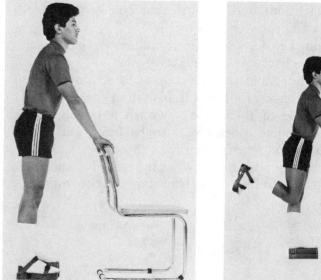

Leg Curl—Start.   Leg Curl—Finish.

Lunges stress the entire thigh, hip, and buttock complex of muscles. They are key movements for reducing and eliminating fatty tissue, particularly when done on a daily basis.

Start in the same position as for a Squat, except that you hold a much lighter barbell across your shoulders. Alternatively, you can hold two light dumbbells at your sides with your arms hanging straight down.

Step forward with your right foot, two-and-a-half to three feet ahead of your left foot. Keeping your torso upright and your left leg straight, slowly bend your right knee as fully as possible. In the bottom position you should feel a stretching sensation in the muscles of your left thigh and right buttock.

Your left knee should be three to five inches above the floor and your right knee should be fully bent and three to five inches ahead of your right ankle.

Recover to the starting position by pushing with your right leg and then bring your feet back together. Repeat the movement by stepping forward with your left foot. Alternate legs for the required number of repetitions for each leg in every set.

Barbell Bent Rowing adds strength, tone, and mass to the large and powerful *latissimus dorsi* muscles of the upper back. Secondary stress is placed on the rear sections of the deltoids and the whole of the biceps.

Set your feet at shoulder width, your toes pointed slightly outward. Unlock your knees five degrees and bend over to take a shoulder-width overgrip on a barbell lying on the floor. Keeping your knees unlocked, arch your back and bring your shoulders upward just enough so the barbell doesn't touch the floor as it hangs at arms' length below your chest.

Slowly bend your arms and pull the barbell upward until it touches the bottom edge of your rib cage. As you pull the bar upward, your upper arm bones should form a 45-degree angle with your torso. Slowly lower the weight back to the starting point and repeat the movement.

Dumbbell Bent Rowing is similar to Barbell Bent Rowing and works the same muscles.

Bend over at the waist and rest your left hand on a flat bench to keep your torso parallel to the floor throughout the movement. Place your left leg two feet ahead of your shoulders and bend it about 30 degrees. Extend your right leg three to three-and-a-half feet to the rear and hold it relatively straight. Finally, grasp a moderately heavy dumbbell in your right hand and fully straighten your arm.

Pull the dumbbell upward until it touches the side of your rib cage, being sure that your upper arm bone travels outward at a 45-degree angle from your chest. Lower the dumbbell back to the starting point. Be sure to perform an equal number of sets and reps for each arm.

The **Stiff-Legged Deadlift** movement strongly stresses the lower back muscles as well as the hamstring muscles along the back of your thighs.

Grasp a barbell with a shoulder-width overgrip and stand erect with your arms straight so that the barbell rests across your upper thighs. Stiffen your legs and bend forward slowly until the barbell plates lightly touch the floor. Slowly return to the starting point and repeat.

If you desire a longer range of motion in this exercise, you should do it while you are standing on a thick block of wood or on the padded surface of a flat exercise bench. This way the barbell plates can't touch the floor and prematurely terminate the movement, and by the time the barbell touches the block or bench surface, your hands will have traveled four to six inches more deeply into the movement than if you had done the exercise standing on the floor. This extra range of motion causes a greater stretch in the hamstrings and lower back muscles.

Upright Rowing is an excellent movement for developing the shoulder, upper back, and biceps muscles. Done on a regular basis, it has a very positive effect on body posture.

Take a narrow overgrip in the middle of a barbell. (A space four to six inches wide should appear between your index fingers.) Straighten your arms and stand erect so the barbell rests across your upper thighs. Then slowly pull the barbell from your thighs up along your body to the under-side of your chin, being certain that your elbows are always higher than your hands as you are pulling. Pause for a second in the top position and slowly lower the barbell back to the starting point. Repeat the movement for the desired number of repetitions.

The **Bench Press** is a super upper body developer. It puts very strong stress on the pectorals, deltoids, and triceps and secondarily stresses the *latissimus dorsi* muscles of the upper back.

(Text continues on page 38.)

Lunge—Start.   Lunge—Finish.

Barbell Bent Rowing—Start.   Barbell Bent Rowing—Finish.

Dumbbell Bent Rowing—Start.   Dumbbell Bent Rowing—Finish.

Stiff-Leg Deadlift—Start.   Stiff-Leg Deadlift—Finish.

Upright Rowing—Start.   Upright Rowing—Finish.

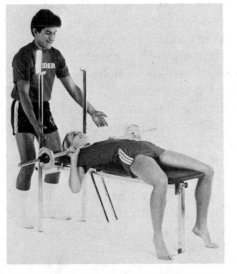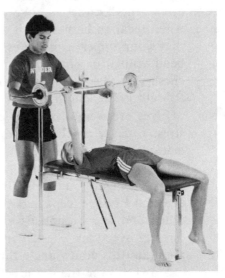

Bench Press—Start (Note Spotter).   Squat—Finish.

Grasp a barbell with an overgrip that places the hands two to three inches wider than your shoulders on each side. Lie back on a flat exercise bench and place your feet flat on the floor directly under your knees. Support the barbell at straight arms' length directly above your shoulder joints.

From this starting point, slowly lower the barbell downward by bending your arms. Be sure that your upper arms travel out at 90-degree angles from your torso as you lower the weight and then press it back up. Lower the weight until it lightly touches the middle of your chest and then steadily push it back to straight arms' length. Repeat the movement for the desired number of repetitions.

The **Incline Press** movement is similar to a Bench Press, except it is done lying on a 45-degree inclined bench rather than on a flat exercise bench. Because of its unique angle, the exercise strongly works the upper edge of the pectorals and the front deltoids.

Take a shoulder-width overgrip on your barbell and lie back on the incline bench. Support the barbell at straight arms' length directly above your shoulder joints. (Your arms will appear to be vertical if viewed from the side.) Being sure that your upper arm bones travel directly out to the sides, bend your arms and lower the barbell until it touches your chest at the base of your neck. Push the weight back to straight arms' length and repeat the movement.

Flyes are weight training exercises that place most of the stress directly on the pectorals, with secondary stress on the deltoids and *latissimus dorsi* muscles.

Grasp two light dumbbells and lie back on a flat exercise bench. Extend your arms directly over your chest as if doing a Bench Press, except that your palms should be facing each other and the dumbbells should lightly touch each other directly over your chest. Bend your elbows 5–10 degrees and maintain this elbow angle throughout the movement.

Slowly lower the dumbbells in semicircles directly out to the sides of your torso until they are below the level of the bench. In the low position of the movement you should feel a stretching sensation in your pectoral muscles. Return the dumbbells back along the same arc you lowered them until they again touch each other above your chest. Repeat the movement for the required number of repetitions.

The **Military Press** is a key shoulder movement, as well as a good triceps, upper chest, and upper back developer. You will recall from our earlier discussion that it is merely the second half of a Clean and Press.

Clean a barbell to your chest and then slowly press it to straight arms' length overhead, being sure it travels upward close to your face. Lower the barbell just back to your shoulders and then immediately press it back overhead. Continue lowering and pressing the weight until your shoulders and arms are comfortably fatigued.

A **Press Behind Neck** is similar to a Military Press, except that the weight is pressed up from behind the neck rather than from in front of it. Presses Behind Neck strongly stress the deltoid, triceps, and trapezius muscles

Clean a barbell to your shoulders and kick a bit with your legs to get the barbell to rest across your shoulders behind your neck. You should still have an overgrip on the bar, but your grip should be two to three inches wider on each side than for a Military Press. Keeping your elbows directly under the barbell handle, press the weight overhead to straight arms' length. Lower back to the starting point and repeat.

Many experienced bodybuilders and weight trainers prefer to do Presses Behind Neck seated on a flat exercise bench. This precludes any assistance by the legs, thereby placing greater stress on the shoulder muscles while handling a lighter weight.

The **Side Lateral Raise** movement places stress almost entirely on the deltoid muscles, particularly on the outer sections.

Grasp two light dumbbells and stand erect. Bend slightly forward at the waist, turn your palms toward each other, and bend your arms 5–10 degrees. Your feet should be about

(Text continues on page 42.)

Incline Press—Start.

Incline Press—Finish.

Flyes—Start.

Flyes—Finish.

Military Press—Start   Military Press—Finish.

Press Behind Neck—Start.   —Finish.

Side Laterals—Start.   Side Laterals—Finish.

shoulder width apart, and the dumbbells will touch in front of your hips. Maintaining your leg and torso position, move only your arms to raise the dumbbells in semicircles from the front of your hips to the level of your shoulders. Throughout the movement, your palms should be facing downward and your arms should be slightly bent. Lower the dumbbells slowly back to the starting point and repeat the movement.

The **Bent Lateral Raise** exercise stresses the upper back muscles and the rear sections of the deltoids.

Hold two dumbbells in your hands. Bend over and slightly unlock your legs. Hang your arms directly below your shoulder joints with your palms facing each other. Bend your arms slightly. From this position, raise the dumbbells to the sides and upward until they are above the level of your shoulders. Slowly lower the dumbbells back to the starting point. Then repeat the movement for the desired number of repetitions.

A **Barbell Curl** develops the biceps muscles along the front of your upper arms as well as the myriad muscles of your forearms.

Take a shoulder-width undergrip on a barbell and stand erect with your arms running down your sides and the barbell resting across your upper thighs. Pin your upper arms to your sides and maintain them in this position throughout the movement. Then, with biceps strength, bend your elbows and slowly move ("curl") the barbell in a semi-circle from your thighs to your chin. Lower back along the same arc to your thighs and repeat the movement. As you curl the barbell up and down, be sure that you do not allow your torso to move back and forth. Your torso should remain bolt upright at all times.

The **Dumbbell Curl** is very similar to a Barbell Curl in that is stresses primarily the biceps muscles and puts secondary stress on the musculature of the forearms.

Grasp two dumbbells in your hands. Stand erect and let your arms hang down at your sides so your palms face each other. Pin your upper arms to the sides of your torso and slowly curl the weights up and down. Note that pronating your hands as you curl provides better biceps stimulation. Pronation involves twisting your wrists so your palms face upward at the conclusion of the curl. Your right thumb, for example, will rotate 90 degrees clockwise as you curl the dumbbell upward.

A **Lying Triceps Extension** is a very good movement for direct triceps stimulation.

Take a narrow overgrip in the middle of a barbell (four to six inches between your index fingers). Lie back on a flat exercise bench and extend your arms directly above your chest in the same position as for the start of a Bench Press, except that you will have taken a narrower grip. Then, keeping your upper arms totally motionless, slowly bend your elbows and lower the barbell in a semicircle from the starting point until it lightly touches your forehead. Use triceps strength to return the weight slowly back to the starting point. Repeat the movement for a whole set.

A **Standing Dumbbell Triceps Extension** also places very direct stress on the triceps muscles along the back of your upper arms.

(Text continues on page 48.)

Bent Laterals—Start.   Bent Laterals—Finish.

Barbell Curl—Start.   Barbell Curl—Finish.

Dumbbell Curl—Start.   Dumbbell Curl—Finish.

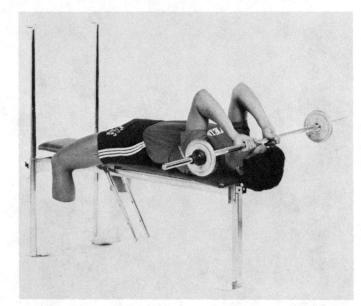

Lying Triceps Extension—Start.

Lying Triceps Extension—Finish.

Dumbbell Triceps Extension—Start. Finish.

In this movement the grip on a single dumbbell with both hands is a key element. When correctly gripped, the dumbbell handle will hang directly downward. Your palms will be placed flat against the underside of the upper set of plates, and your thumbs will encircle the dumbbell handle to keep the weight secure in your hands as you do the movement.

Once you have a firm grip on the dumbbell, stand erect and extend your arms directly overhead. Your upper arms should be pressed against the sides of your head, and they should remain there throughout the movement. Slowly bend your elbows and lower the dumbbell in a semicircle to a point as low down your back as possible. Then use triceps strength to return the weight slowly back to the starting point. Repeat the movement for the required number of repetitions.

A **Barbell Reverse Curl** is the same movement as a Barbell Curl, except you use an overgrip instead of an undergrip. Reverse Curls stimulate the forearm, biceps, and *brachialis* muscles.

Take a shoulder-width overgrip on a barbell. Stand erect with your feet set at shoulder width and run your arms down the sides of your body so the barbell rests across your upper thighs. Press your upper arms against the sides of your torso and leave them in this position throughout the movement. Then slowly curl the weight in a semicircle from your thighs to your chin. Lower back to the starting point and repeat. Be sure that your torso remains motionless as you curl the weight up and down.

A **Barbell Wrist Curl** develops the muscles of your forearms. Done with your palms facing upward, it stresses the muscles on your inner forearms. Done palms down, Wrist Curls develop the muscles of the outside of your forearms.

Let's illustrate and describe Wrist Curls done with palms up, and then you can use the same directions to do the palms-down version. Take an undergrip on a barbell (with about 12–14 inches between your hands). Sit on the edge of a flat exercise bench with your feet set 12–14 inches apart. Then run your forearms down your thighs so your fists hang off the edges of your knees.

Sag your fists downward as far as possible. Then slowly curl the barbell upward in a small semicircle by fully flexing your wrists. Slowly lower the weight back to the starting point and repeat the movement for the desired number of reps.

The **Wrist Roller** exercise is an easy way to develop all the forearm muscles.

Take a narrow overgrip on the wrist roller handle, stand erect, and extend your arms straight out ahead of your shoulders so they are parallel to the floor. Then simply roll the cord holding the weight up on the dowel, first in one direction and then in the other.

If you don't have a wrist roller, you can easily improvise. Go to a hardware or lumber store and buy a dowel that is 14–16 inches long and one-and-a-quarter to one-and-a-half inches thick. Drill a hole one-quarter to three-eighths inch in diameter crosswise through the thickest part of the dowel and in the middle of its length. Run a four- to four-and-a-half-foot length of clothesline through the hole and make a large knot in one end of it to keep the rope from coming back through the hole. Finally, tie a dumbbell to the other end of your rope and you have a homemade wrist roller.

The **Standing Calf Raise** develops the gastrocnemius and soleus muscles along the backs of your lower legs.

You will need a piece of four-by-four-inch board about 12–16 inches long for all calf exercises. You will achieve a greater range of motion while working your calves if you stand with your toes on such a block and force your heels below the level of your toes on each repetition. To keep your block from rolling, nail a thin piece of plywood to the bottom of it.

Place a barbell across your shoulders in the same manner as you would to start a Squat. Put your toes and the balls of

(Text continues on page 52.)

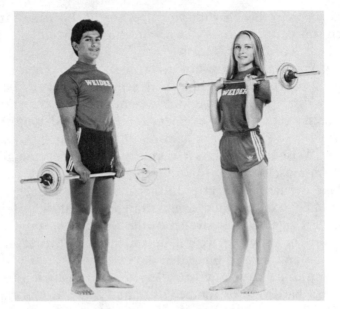

Reverse Curl—Start.   Reverse Curl—Finish.

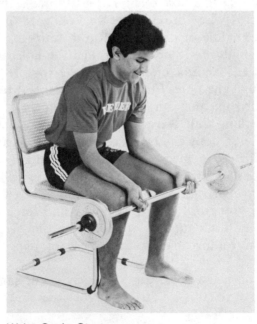

Wrist Curl—Start.

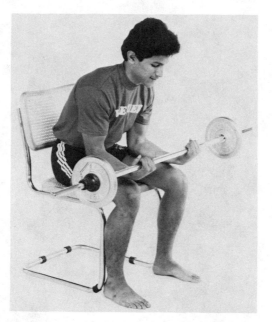

Wrist Curl—Finish.

Wrist Curl with Reverse Grip.

Wrist Roller.

Standing Calf Raise—Start.   Standing Calf Raise—Finish.

your feet on the block and lock your knees. Then sag your heels well below your toes and slowly rise as high as possible on your toes and the balls of your feet. Sag back down and repeat the movement for a full set.

On all calf exercises you should alternately use three toe positions—toes pointed outward 45 degrees, toes pointed straight ahead, and toes pointed inward about 45 degrees. Each of these toe positions affects the calf muscles somewhat differently, and all should be used to strengthen and develop your calves fully.

A **Seated Calf Raise** stresses all the calf muscles, but particularly the wide, thin soleus muscle lying under the gastrocnemius.

Load up a heavy barbell and then wrap a thick towel around the middle of its handle. You will need this padding, because the barbell will rest across your knees during the movement.

Place the barbell on your knees and sit at the edge of a flat exercise bench. Put your toes and the balls of your feet on your wooden block. Then simply rise up and sink down on your toes as in a Standing Calf Raise. Be sure to use all three toe positions previously mentioned for each succeeding set.

Sit-Ups strengthen, tone, and flatten the muscles of your frontal abdomen, particularly the upper half of the frontal abdominals.

Lie on your back on the floor and hook your toes under a barbell that is lying on the floor. Bend your legs about 30 degrees, because straight-legged Sit-Ups can injure your lower back. Interlace your fingers behind your neck. Slowly raise your head from the floor, then your shoulders, upper back, and lower back, until your torso makes a right angle with your legs. Slowly lower back to the starting point and repeat for the required number of repetitions.

There is a special abdominal board for Sit-Ups. The higher you raise the foot end of this board, the more difficult the exercise becomes.

Leg Raises strengthen and flatten the frontal abdominal muscles. They particularly stress the lower half of the frontal abdomen.

Lie on your back on the floor and grasp a heavy piece of furniture or a barbell behind your head to steady your body during the movement. Bend your legs 10–15 degrees. Raise your legs upward so your feet travel in a semicircle from the floor to a position directly above your hips. Lower back to the starting point and repeat the movement.

Leg Raises can also be done on the abdominal board that is used for Sit-Ups. Your head will be at the top end of the board, however.

Side Bends tone and strengthen the muscles at the sides of your waist.

(Text continues on page 57.)

Seated Calf Raise—Start.

Seated Calf Raise—Finish.

Sit-Up—Start.

Sit-Up—Finish.

Leg Raises—Start.

Leg Raises—Finish.

Side Bend—Start.   Side Bend—Finish.

Place an unloaded barbell or a broomstick across your shoulders and behind your neck. Grasp the barbell or broomstick with each hand out toward the ends. Spread your feet two to two-and-a-half feet apart and hold your legs straight for the entire movement. Stand erect. Bend your torso directly to the left side as far as possible, return to an erect position, and bend your torso directly to the right side as far as you can. Rhythmically bend back and forth from side to side for the required number of repetitions. Count a full cycle to the right and left as one repetition.

The **Seated Twisting** movement tones the muscles at the sides of your waist.

Sit down on a flat exercise bench and wrap your legs

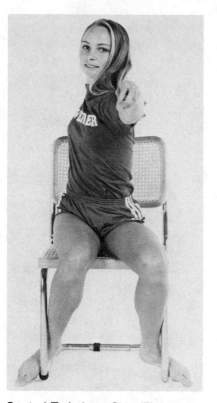 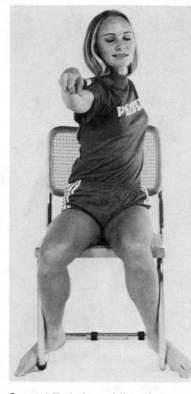

Seated Twisting—Start/Finish.   Seated Twisting—Midpoint.

around the legs of the bench to restrain your hips and legs from moving during the exercise. Place an unloaded barbell or broomstick across your shoulders and behind your neck. Wrap your arms around the bar or stick. Then twist your shoulders and torso forcefully as far as you can to the left. Immediately twist as far as you can to the right. Twist rhythmically from side to side for the required number of reps, counting each full cycle to the left and right as one repetition.

Various **Neck Strap** movements will shape and strengthen all the neck muscles.

Attach a light barbell plate to the headstrap chain and put the harness over your head so the weight dangles down in

Neck Strap—Start.   Neck Strap—Finish.

front of your chest. Sit at the end of a flat exercise bench and lean forward about 15–20 degrees from the vertical position. Place your hands on your thighs to steady your body in this position. Then move your head forward and downward until your chin touches your chest. Then pull your head backward as far as you can. Lower back to your chest and repeat the movement. This develops the muscles on the back and sides of your neck.

By running the chain and weight down your back and leaning slightly backward, you can do the same movement so it stresses muscles on the front and sides of your neck.

4

Training Routines

It's now time to combine the training tips from Chapter 2 and the exercises from Chapter 3 to form actual training routines that you can use to improve your appearance, strength, health, and physical fitness. Here is a very basic routine that beginners can use for the first four to six weeks of training. Remember that the columns labeled "% Men" and "% Women" indicate the weights you should use in terms of percentages of your body weight.

Exercise	Sets	Reps	% Men	% Women
1. Clean and Press	1	10–15	30	20
2. Squat	3	10–15	40	30
3. Barbell Bent Rowing	3	8–12	35	25
4. Upright Rowing	2	8–12	30	20
5. Bench Press	3	6–10	35	25
6. Military Press	2	6–10	30	20
7. Barbell Curl	3	8–12	30	20

Exercise	Sets	Reps	% Men	% Women
8. Lying Triceps Extension	2–3	8–12	25	15
9. Barbell Wrist Curl	2	15–20	25	15
10. Standing Calf Raise	3	15–20	40	30
11. Sit-Ups	1	20–30	——	——

Remember to train on three nonconsecutive days per week and break in slowly as suggested in Chapter 2. Also, don't worry about the lack of neck exercises in this beginning routine. At this level, your neck will gain tone and strength from exercises like Upright Rowing and Military Presses, which stress muscles peripheral to the neck.

Next, you can use this more intense routine on three nonconsecutive days per week for the next four to six weeks:

Exercise	Sets	Reps
1. Clean and Press	1	10–15
2. Squat	4	10–15
3. Iron Boot Leg Curl	2	8–12
4. Stiff-Legged Deadlift	1	10–15
5. Dumbbell Bent Rowing	4	8–12
6. Upright Rowing	3	8–12
7. Incline Press	3	6–10
8. Flyes	2	8–12
9. Press Behind Neck	3	6–10
10. Side Lateral Raise	2	8–12
11. Dumbbell Curl	4	8–12
12. Standing Dumbbell Triceps Extension	4	8–12
13. Reverse Curl	3	8–12
14. Wrist Roller	3	——
15. Leg Raises	2–3	25–50
16. Side Bends	2–3	50–100
17. Seated Calf Raise	4–5	12–15

This is a pretty stiff routine, so take about two weeks to work up to it from the first training program. Then stay on the second routine for another four to six weeks.

Your third beginning-level weight training routine will be quite intense, and it should take about an hour to an hour and 15 minutes to complete.

Exercise	Sets	Reps
1. Clean and Press	1	10–15
2. Lunges	3	10–15
3. Iron Boot Leg Extension	3	10–15
4. Iron Boot Leg Curl	3	8–12
5. Stiff-Legged Deadlift	1	10–15
6. Barbell Bent Rowing	3	8–12
7. Dumbbell Bent Rowing	2–3	8–12
8. Upright Rowing	2	8–12
9. Incline Press	3	6–10
10. Bench Press	3	6–10
11. Press Behind Neck	2	6–10
12. Side Lateral Raise	2	8–12
13. Bent Lateral Raise	2	8–12
14. Barbell Curl	2	8–12
15. Dumbbell Curl	2	8–12
16. Lying Triceps Extension	3	8–12
17. Standing Dumbbell Triceps Extension	2	8–12
18. Reverse Curl	3	8–12
19. Wrist Curl	3	15–20
20. Standing Calf Raise	3	15–20
21. Seated Calf Raise	3	10–15
22. Neck Strap	3	8–10
23. Sit-Ups	2–3	25–50
24. Seated Twisting	2–3	50–100

If you survive four to six weeks of this type of difficult weight training, you have graduated from the ranks of beginners to the intermediate level. And if you still enjoy pumping iron, you've probably been bitten by the iron bug and will have iron fever for life!

Some men and women decide that they would like to concentrate on developing maximum strength. Generally speaking, strength is a function less of muscle size than of connective tissue (tendons and ligaments) strength and the ability to recruit a maximum number of muscle fibers on each lift. To develop these two qualities, it is necessary to do basic exercises (defined in Chapter 5) for each body part; do five to eight total sets per exercise, using very heavy weights; and perform low repetitions of each set, in the range of one to three reps following a thorough warm-up.

To achieve this type of warm-up and low-rep training, we use a set-rep system called *pyramidding* in which the weight is increased and the reps decreased with each succeeding set. Here is a typical pyramidding scheme (100 percent of maximum is the highest weight with which you can do one strict movement in any exercise):

Set Number	Reps	Percent of Maximum
1	8	50
2	6	65
3	4	80
4	3	85–90
5	2	90–95
6	1	95–100

Using this pyramidding scheme, here is a good power-building routine that you can do three times per week. Pyramid the sets and reps for the exercises marked with asterisks.

Exercise	Sets	Reps
1. Sit-Ups	2–3	25–50
2. Squats*	5	8/6/4/3/2
3. Stiff-Legged Deadlift*	3	8/6/4
4. Barbell Bent Rowing*	5	10/8/6/5/4
5. Upright Rowing*	3	8/6/4
6. Bench Press*	5	8/6/4/3/2
7. Military Press*	3	6/4/2
8. Barbell Curl*	3	8/6/4
9. Lying Triceps Extension*	3	8/6/4
10. Barbell Wrist Curl	3	10–15
11. Seated Calf Raise	2–3	8–10
12. Standing Calf Raise	2–3	10–15

5

Intermediate Techniques

In this chapter I will explain several of the more advanced, beginning training techniques which would probably have confused you had they been presented earlier in the book. As an example, it would be difficult to fully understand the concept of training to failure in a set unless you already had trained fairly hard for several weeks and pushed some of your sets either to the point, or almost to the point, where your working muscles became too fatigued to allow you to complete a full repetition. I will also explain several factors related to weight training (such as overtraining) that simply wouldn't apply to a beginner.

THE SECRETS

It has long been said that there are no secrets in weight training and bodybuilding. There are, however, two secrets to success in these activities—patience and consistency.

Results from weight training come fairly steadily but very

slowly, particularly for women (remember, their hormonal makeup prevents great gains in strength and muscle mass). Therefore, you must be persistent in your weight training if you are to succeed ultimately.

You must also be consistent. Missing workouts not only prevents you from making progress, but can actually set you back. Each missed workout sets you back two workouts. It takes one training session to regain the condition you had attained before missing a workout. Then you must do one more workout to begin making progress again.

TRAINING PARTNERS

Once you are past the pure beginning level of weight training, it is often valuable and pleasurable to have a training partner. Such a partner can spot you in a number of exercises, particularly in Bench Presses. And a training partner can offer you a certain degree of camaraderie. It's less likely that you will miss a workout if someone else is sitting at the gym expecting you to show up.

TRAINING TO FAILURE

Up until this point I have recommended that you terminate each set at the point when you begin to feel comfortably fatigued. For maximum results in developing strength and muscle mass, however, you should "train to failure" on one or two sets of each exercise.

Training to failure merely involves continuing a set until you are literally unable to complete a full repetition of a movement. For example, after seven or eight reps of a Military Press, your final repetition stalls out just above head height. Try as you will, you can't push it any higher. That's training to failure.

On some exercises, such as Bench Presses and Squats, it's necessary to use a training partner or two when training to failure. This will keep you from being pinned under the barbell once you fail to complete a repetition.

OVERTRAINING

It is possible to overtax the body and mind by doing workouts that are too lengthy. In that case you become overtrained and cease to make progress. It becomes an ordeal just to go into the gym to work out.

Newcomers to weight training should do no more than four to five total sets for each muscle group, while intermediates should not exceed six to eight sets per body part. Going past these totals pushes the body so hard that it doesn't have time to recuperate fully before the next workout is upon you. And that is what leads to overtraining.

How can you tell if you are overtrained? There are five distinct symptoms:

1. Chronic fatigue, frequent colds and other infections
2. Apathy toward doing workouts
3. Insomnia
4. Persistently sore muscles and/or joints
5. Elevated morning pulse rate

If you exhibit one or more of these symptoms, you should take a one-week layoff from training to allow your body time to recuperate fully. Then you should return to weight training but do 20–25% fewer total sets for each body part than you were doing before you overtrained. Don't train as long, but train harder, and you'll make optimum progress without overtraining.

INJURIES

Participants in every athletic activity suffer muscle and/or joint injuries from time to time. If an injury is painful when you do a weight training exercise that stresses it, simply avoid doing that movement for a week or two until the pain subsides. Later, as you gain more experience with weight training, you will be able to choose exercises that allow you to "train around an injury."

If you have been seriously injured and the injury has healed, weight training can be a valuable tool for rehabilitating atrophied muscles in and around the injury. In this case, weight training should be undertaken only with the direction of your physician or a qualified physical therapist. And you should promptly cease if you feel any pain in the injured area.

Despite the heavy nature of the activity, it is very difficult actually to injure yourself while training with weights. To avoid injury, simply use the correct biomechanical (body) positionings recommended for each exercise in Chapter 3. And never do any weight training exercise in a jerky manner. Follow these suggestions—being sure to keep warm while working out—and you'll probably never be injured while training with weights.

SPORTS IMPROVEMENT

Weight training dramatically improves performance in any sport. That is why virtually all athletes now train with weights. All the weight training programs listed in Chapter 4 will improve your sports performance. Or, if you want to work out with a routine tailored to your particular sport, consult one of my earlier books, the *Complete Weight Training Book* (Anderson-World, 1976), which includes a large number of these.

BASIC vs. ISOLATION EXERCISES

Basic exercises are those that work large muscle groups like the chest or back in conjunction with smaller muscles like the arms. Typical basic exercises are Squats (thighs and lower back), Bench Presses (pectorals, deltoids, and triceps), Barbell Bent Rowing (*latissimus dorsi* and biceps), and Military Presses (deltoids and triceps).

Isolation exercises work one muscle group, and sometimes even only a part of a muscle group, in relative isolation from the rest of the body. Typical isolation exercises are Leg Curls (hamstrings), Leg Extensions (quadriceps), Side Lateral Raises (deltoids), and Lying or Standing Triceps Extensions (triceps).

Generally speaking, since basic exercises work large muscle groups with heavy weights, they are used to build strength and muscle mass. Isolation movements, in contrast, are usually used in injury rehabilitation and by bodybuilders who seek to shape and refine the appearance of individual muscle groups.

NAUTILUS AND UNIVERSAL GYMS

While this book is concerned with training with free weights—barbells, dumbbells, and related equipment—I do not deny the existence and value of exercise machines. Indeed, I feel that Nautilus, Universal Gyms, and other machines—although too expensive for home-gym training— are excellent pieces of equipment for use in heavy resistance training.

Machines are superior to free weights in three ways. First, they offer variable resistance. When using a barbell for a Bench Press, the weight begins to feel light over the last half of the movement, because the chest, shoulder, and arm muscles have been brought into position where they can exert far more pressure against the weight (e.g., into what is called a more favorable "mechanical position") than they could earlier in the movement. Literally, you can push much more weight over the last half of the movement than over the first half. Exercise machines are usually constructed to make the resistance heavier over parts of the movements in which your muscles are in their strongest mechanical position.

Second, many machines—particularly Nautilus—offer rotary resistance. When you do a Barbell Curl the weight feels heaviest only when your forearms are at right angles to your upper arms, because only then are you exerting muscular force directly against the pull of gravity. This is not true at the start or finish of a Barbell Curl. Exercise machines are constructed with pulleys and lever arms that effectively "rotate" gravity about an axis, so you are always pulling or pushing directly against the force of gravity. Hence, the weight feels heavy along the full range of motion of an exercise.

Thirdly, and crucially, all of the exercise machines with which I am familiar—including both Nautilus and Universal Gyms machines—are constructed to fully protect a trainee from injury if he or she is forced to train alone. In other words, they can be used in total safety without a spotter standing by. Let me give you an example of how this safety factor works in actual practice.

As you will recall from reading my section on safety in Chapter 2, when you do Bench Presses with a heavy weight, you can either get stuck with the barbell across your chest, or (very rarely) pass out while pressing it up, making you open to serious injury. This is why you do heavy Bench Presses only when a spotter is standing by.

On Nautilus and Universal Gyms machines, however, you press a weight that is mechanically restricted to the same movement arc on every repetition. There will be no bar crossing your chest, and you press the weight from your chest on the initial repetition of each set. Therefore, if you can't get a weight up, you simply walk away from the machine, because the weight is in its normal resting position when at chest level. And if you faint while pressing the weight, it will fall harmlessly back to its normal resting postition without contacting any part of your body besides your hands.

There are two primary drawbacks to resistance machines. First, they are extremely expensive. A Universal Gyms machine costs a minimum of $3,500, while a *complete* barbell gym would cost less than $200. A home-gym installation of Nautilus machines sufficient to train the whole body would cost more than $50,000! Even a year's membership dues to a Nautilus club will average $300 per year, 50% more than the cost of a complete barbell gym that you can use for life. Clearly, it is much more economical to train with free weights.

Second, you can do only three to five exercises per muscle group on resistance machines. Many Nautilus machines allow only one exercise to be done. In contrast, there are more than 100 different movements that can be done with free weights for most body parts. And the fewer exercises you do for a muscle group, the more easily you will become bored with your workouts.

If you are a member of a health club or gym, you will probably have access to heavy resistance machines. In that case, you will quickly discover that you will be able to do optimum workouts when you use a *combination* of machines and free weights in your training sessions.

OPTIMUM PHYSICAL FITNESS

Optimum physical fitness includes strength, endurance, and body flexibility. Obviously, weight training will give you considerable strength, but you must do other types of physical training to develop endurance and flexibility.

Stretching is the best route to body flexibility. For optimum results, stretching should be done almost every day, so I recommend doing it as part of your warm-up for either weight training or aerobic exercise. Only five or ten minutes per day of stretching will eventually result in a high degree of flexibility, but it will take several months of regular stretching workouts to reach this point.

You can find good stretching exercises and stretching programs in two books available in most bookstores: *Stretching* by Bob Anderson and *The Complete Stretching Book* by Paul Uram.

Aerobic exercise promotes endurance, and when most individuals think of aerobics they think of running. There are, however, numerous other types of aerobic exercise that you can include in your endurance program. These include playing handball or racquet sports, swimming, bicycling, walking, mountain climbing and hiking, dancing, and rowing. Try a different one of these aerobic activities each day, and I'm sure you'll always find your interest at a maximum.

If you desire optimum fitness, do your weight training workouts on Mondays, Wednesdays, and Fridays. And do aerobic training sessions on Tuesdays, Thursdays, and Saturdays, perhaps on Sundays too. Stretch before both your weight workouts and aerobic sessions. And in two or three months you'll be in tremendous physical condition!

INDIVIDUALIZED ROUTINES

Ultimately, you will outgrow the training routines outlined in Chapter 4. Then you can turn to some of the intermediate and advanced training techniques and routines contained in the books mentioned in the "Moving On" section at the end of the next chapter. Or, you can learn to make up your own routines.

Here are six guidelines you can use when making up your own more advanced training routines from the exercises in Chapter 4.

1. Train four days per week on a split routine: Work your chest, shoulders, upper arms, forearms, calves, and abdominals on Mondays and Thursdays. On Tuesdays and Fridays, do exercises for your thighs, back, calves, and abdominals.

2. Do no more than six to eight total sets (use one or two exercises) for your back, thighs, and chest. Do four to six total sets for your shoulders, biceps, triceps, forearms, calves, and abdominals.

3. Always do your torso (chest, back, and shoulders) exercises before your arm (biceps and triceps) movements. Always do forearm exercises last in your routine.

4. You can do your abdominal and/or calf training first in your workout as a warm-up for your weight training program for the rest of your body.

5. Stay on one routine for only four to six weeks before switching to another.

6. As you encounter new exercises for various muscle groups, give each a four- to six-week trial in your routine. All weight trainers and bodybuilders find that some exercises work better for them than others. All bodies are different.

6

Sources—Equipment and References

In this chapter, I will tell you where to buy weight training equipment, as well as what types of equipment you should purchase for your own home gym. I will also give you a number of sources for additional information on weight training that will make it easy for you to decide in which direction to go once you've completed the training routines outlined in this book.

EQUIPPING A GYM

Assuming that you don't join an organized gym, you will need to obtain equipment for a home gym. At a minimum you will need to buy an adjustable barbell-dumbbell set. For starters, a woman could do quite well with a 90-pound set (cost: about $50 new). Men would need a 110-pound set for starters (about $70 new). Then, as you grow too strong for your starter set, you can upgrade it by buying additional plates.

Actually, there is no need to purchase a new weight set, because numerous, slightly used sets are available at garage sales. As I mentioned in Chapter 2, the sets with metal plates are preferable to those with plates made of vinyl-covered concrete.

You might even be able to pick up an adjustable exercise bench at a garage sale. If not, you can buy one for as little as $40–$50, or for a king's ransom, depending on the quality of the equipment. These benches are quite convenient, and they're virtually a necessity to any serious beginning weight trainer.

Gradually, you can add other pieces of equipment that will make your training more enjoyable and productive. Of course each piece of equipment will cost a few dollars, but such expenditures are one-time outlays versus yearly gym dues.

Large department stores and many sporting goods stores sell weight training equipment. The following large equipment companies have catalogs of products that they sell.

Weider Health & Fitness
21100 Erwin St.
Woodland Hills, CA 91367

Body Culture Equipment Co.
PO Box 10
Alliance, NE 69301

Dan Lurie
1665 Utica Ave.
Brooklyn, NY 11234

Robert Kennedy
Unit One
270 Rutherford Rd. S.
Brampton, Ont. L6W 3K7
Canada

Marcy
1736 Standard Ave.
Glendale, CA 91201

Billard Barbell Co.
208 Chestnut St.
Reading, PA 19602

York Barbell Co.
PO Box 1707
York, PA 17405

Ed Jubinville
PO Box 662
Holyoke, MA 01040

Tennessee Gym Equipment
PO Box 5847
Knoxville, TN 37918

Bell Foundry
PO Box 1070
Southgate, CA 90806

Paramount
3000 South Santa Fe Ave.
Los Angeles, CA 90058

Mav-Rik
3916 Eagle Rock Blvd.
Los Angeles, CA 90065

MOVING ON

A few men and women who have followed the programs outlined in this book will decide that pumping iron is not for them, and they will drop out. The rest will move on past the beginners' stage to specialize in one form of the iron game or another.

The first alternative is to use weight training merely to keep healthy and stay in good shape. If that is your goal, I suggest that you read *Boyer & Valerie Coe's Weight Training Book* (Contemporary Books, 1982). This fine and very complete book covers all aspects of training for health, fitness, and even bodybuilding competition.

As I mentioned earlier, athletes can follow specialized weight training programs geared to their own sports. They should read the *Complete Weight Training Book* (Anderson-World, 1976) for these types of sports improvement programs.

Competitive weight lifting and powerlifting also attract both men and women. There are two fine books that you can read about these activities: Dr. Fred Hatfield's *Powerlifting—A Scientific Approach* (Contemporary Books, 1981) and Dr. Franco Columbu's *Winning Weight Lifting and Powerlifting* (Contemporary Books, 1981).

Bodybuilding beckons to thousands of men and women. The best books on this sport are Joe Weider's *Bodybuilding: The Weider Approach* (Contemporary Books, 1981) and *The Weider Book of Bodybuilding for Women* (Contemporary Books, 1981) by Betty and Joe Weider. Also quite good is Dr. Franco Columbu's *Winning Bodybuilding* (Contemporary Books, 1977). And you definitely should read the monthly bodybuilding magazine *Muscle & Fitness*, the bible of the sport. It's available at all large newsstands.

THE DECISION IS YOURS

I have taken you, as beginners, as far as I can in this book. It's now up to you to start training, whether at home or in a gym. I heartily hope you stick with weight training, because it will make you look and feel better—and you may find that some of the most enjoyable moments of your day are spent in the gym. Once you've achieved a good pump in a workout, you'll be after it for the rest of your life.

Index

Isolation exercises, 71
Leg Curls, 71
Leg Extensions, 71
Leg Raises, 53, 56
Lunges, 32–33, 35
Lying Triceps Extension, 43, 46, 71

M

Mental aspects, of weight
    training, 23
Military Press, 28, 29, 41, 71
Mixed grip, definition of, 12
Movement, 11
Mr. America, 16
Muscle & Fitness, 80
Muscle hypertrophy, 4–5
Muscle physiology, 4–6

N, O

Nautilus gyms, 71–73
Neck Strap movements, 73–74
Nutrition, 22–23
Optimum physical fitness, 73–74
Overgrip, 12
Overtraining, 69

P

Physical exams, need for, before
    starting weight training,
    13–14
Poundages, 19
Power Clean, 28
*Powerlifting—A Scientific
    Approach* (Hatfield), 20
Press Behind Neck, 39, 41
Program, 12
Progression, 14–16

Q, R

Repetition, 12, 20
Rest interval, 12
    importance of, 16
Rest. *See* Sleep/rest
Routines
    changing of, 26
    definition of, 12
    individualized, 74–75
Safety
    and injuries, 69–70
    in weight training, 25–26
Seated Calf Raise, 52–53, 54
Seated Twist, 57–58
Set, 12
Side Bends, 53, 57
Side Lateral Raise, 39, 42, 71
Sit-Ups, 53, 55
Sleep/rest, 21–22
Split routine, 17
Sports improvement, 70
Spotter, 25, 72
Squat, 5, 12, 24, 28, 30, 68, 71
Standing Calf Raise, 49, 52
Standing Dumbbell Triceps
    Extension, 43, 47, 48, 71
Starting weights, 19–20
Stiff-Leg Deadlift, 34, 36
Stretching, 73–74
Stretching (Anderson), 74

T

Training frequency, 16–17
Training partners, 68
Training program, 12
Training routines, 61–65
Training speed, 16
Training to failure, 68–69

U, V

Undergrip, 12
Universal gyms, 71–73
Upright Rowing, 34, 37
Uram, Paul, 74

W–Z

Warm-ups, 24, 25
*Weider Book of Bodybuilding
  for Women,* 80
Weider, Betty, 80
Weider, Joe, 80
Weight lifting, 3
Weight lifting belt, 19, 26
Weight training
  advantages of, 8
  age factor in, 9
  beauty of, 10
  beginning in, 2–3
  breaking in, 23–24
  and breathing, 21
  changing routines in, 26
  clothing for, 18–19
  definition of, 3
  disadvantages of, 7–8
  exercise form, 20–21
  frequency, 16–17

importance of nutrition, 22–23
importance of sleep/rest,
  21–22
intermediate techniques, 67–75
location for, 17–18
men versus women, 8–9
mental aspects of, 23
myths regarding, 6–7
number of repetitions, 20
overtraining in, 69
physical and mental results of,
  1–2
safety in, 25–26, 69–70
secrets to success in, 67–68
speed, 16–17
starting weights for, 19–20
timing of, 17
training partners, 68
types of, 3–4
use of weight lifting belts, 19
warm-ups, 24
Winning Bodybuilding
  (Columbu), 80
Winning Weight Lifting
  (Columbu), 80
Women, weight training for, 6,
  8–9
Workout, 12
Wrist Roller, 49